helping young people

Naked Christianity

CRIS ROGERS

kevin **mayhew**

First published in 2004 by
KEVIN MAYHEW LTD
Buxhall, Stowmarket, Suffolk, IP14 3BW
E-mail: info@kevinmayhewltd.com

9 8 7 6 5 4 3 2 1 0

ISBN 1 84417 341 0
Catalogue No. 1500748

Cover design by Angela Selfe
Edited and typeset by Katherine Laidler
Illustrations by 'Son'

Printed and bound in Great Britain

*With thanks to Beki, an amazing wife and friend,
thanks for all the fun and laughter. And to Isaac,
you are all your mummy and daddy could ever wish for!*

If you want to see a good example of Evangelism and Ministry to young people, go and see what Cris Rogers is doing at 'The Gathering' Youth Congregation, Birmingham. If you cannot get to Birmingham, read this book. It is full of good sense and stimulating stories and creative ideas. Helping young people to catch the vision of who Jesus Christ is must be our number one priority for the Body of Christ. Reading Cris' book you can't help but catch the vision and have fun too. If you want a fantastic starting point with the Christian faith, this is the book to read. Have you caught the vision yet?

*THE RT REVD DR JOHN SENTAMU,
THE BISHOP OF BIRMINGHAM*

Cris Rogers is a Christian youth worker doing innovative work. Cris has put together some of the most common questions asked him by young people over the years and, guess what? He's answered them in a lively and straightforward way. It would be wrong to claim that *Naked Christianity* offers the last word on these subjects, but it does represent an excellent starting point.

*STEVE TILLEY,
HEAD OF CHURCH YOUTH FELLOWSHIP ASSOCIATION
1994 - 2002, AND FREELANCE WRITER*

CONTENTS

Naked (nkid)

adj.

1. Having no clothing on the body

2. Having no covering, especially the
   usual one

a. Devoid of vegetation, trees or foliage:
   the naked ground; naked tree limbs

b. Being without addition, concealment,
   disguise or embellishment

3. To see clearly what is underneath

a. Devoid of anything that will distract
   you from the truth: a look that was naked
   of all pretences

4. Exposed

5. Lacking outer covering such as fur,
   feathers or a shell

6. Having no means of defence or
   protection; open; unarmed; defenceless

7. Mere; simple; plain

INTRODUCTION

Naked Christianity started after an amazing evening on a youth week-end away. We spent the evening writing out our questions and thoughts on large sheets of paper. The next day we spent time answering each other's questions, jotting down ideas and views and praying with each other. The same questions came out again and again. It was as if those same questions are programmed within us:

Is it OK to question God?
Does God really care enough to answer our prayers?
Why is there suffering?

The goal of this book is to help young people grasp issues about faith. This could be done by a single reader using the questions at the end of each chapter to help them think through the issues themselves. Or the book could be used in a small group setting by using the questions and scripture suggestions at the end of each chapter to discuss and think through the issues together. You can read it alone or with a friend, study with it, talk about it or just use it as a fan on those warm summer nights!

The book brings together a range of the questions most frequently asked by teenagers and introduces ideas and concepts to think about and to be challenged by over the chapters. In no way are all possible points covered within the book – they aren't intended to be – but this book's a place to start and to think about what we believe as Christians and how God wants to relate to us. Please don't get me wrong and think that I've got all the answers. I question constantly; it's a journey, a walk with our Maker. All I know is that God will give us the answers we need and will carry us on the road.

God loves a quizzical mind that is walking and chatting with him over a mind that thinks it knows all and never even jumps on the road. I hope that this book helps you strip away some of the outer clothing of Christianity, so that you can leave behind some misconceptions and jump on the road and spend some time getting a few glimpses of the answers.

QUESTION 1
Can we really ask questions?

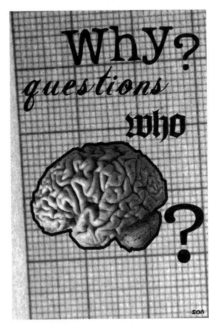

Did you know that the average 5-year-old asks between 23 and 34 questions a day? Wow! I'm just dreading the day when, as a father, I have to answer all those questions – if my maths is correct that's around 10,000 a year. I mean, how can there be so many questions in the world?

Game madness

The thing is, we all have questions but we all react differently to being asked them. I have a brother named Tim who is four years younger than me. Now, Tim is a great guy and I would never swap him for the world for another brother: he is funny, handsome and extremely brainy, although he doesn't choose to show this very often.

But he hasn't always been like this. I remember when I was only 12 and he was 8, we loved the film *Ghost Busters* and the second movie had just come out. As we know, with all good movies comes the merchandise: comics, T-shirts, lunch boxes, hats, toys and cartoons. For a young teenager the computer game of the film is the most important bit of the movie merchandise and you will queue for hours to get a copy. So I queued and queued to get a copy of *Ghost Busters 2* for my Commodore 64. I saved for weeks and finally I had it in my hands. Before PCs and Macs, and well before Gameboys and PS2s, you had a game that came on a cassette tape. They would take hours to load and on many occasions would never load at all.

But I was confident this was not going to happen. I slid the cassette in the computer cassette recorder and set it loading. You could sit for what felt like light years waiting for the game to appear. Now this was where my story went downhill. My little brother, aged 8, entered the room.

'What are you doing?'

'I'm playing.'

The questions started and over the next 10 minutes I must have had over the 30-question limit. Why? Why? Why? I could feel the blood pressure rising and rising and rising, and to top it off the tape in the cassette player started to chew. I could hear it squealing in front of me. I quickly stopped the machine and started to try and rewind the tape back into the cassette using a pen, when more questions started.

'What's the matter?'

'What's happened?'

'Why are you playing with the tape?'

'Can I have a go first?'

My face was now bright red and ready to go pop, and still more questions appeared. I had had enough. Very slowly I reached down to my left, just behind my computer desk where I kept a pillow and slowly laid it on my lap. I then, again very slowly, reached down to my side where I kept the biggest joystick in history. It was a pilot's joystick, one with loads of dials and knobs and a flip-up fire button; this thing was huge and very heavy.

I slowly started to wrap the joystick up in the pillow and turned to my brother.

'What are you doing? Why do you have a joystick in a pillow?'

Like the Terminator I slowly said to him, 'Do you want me to show you?'

And so I stretched out my right arm and without hesitation I started to swing. The joystick and pillow smacked my brother in the face and threw him across the room, making him hit my wardrobe five metres away and knocking his front tooth out, and I swear I could hear him ask:

'What are you doing?'

We all ask questions: some of us ask them all the time and some of us ask them only when we have to. Most of us like to think that we already know the answers. We also react differently to how we answer questions: some of us love answering hundreds of questions and others, like me, hate more than a handful at one time. Unlike Jesus, I would not answer the questions I was given. (By the way, Tim, I would like to say sorry publicly for my burst of rage!)

Many of us have been encouraged to think that to ask questions shows a deep weakness, not only in our lives but also in our personal faith. However, the Bible is full of people who questioned their faith and others who questioned God.

Questioners in the Bible

Right at the beginning of the Bible, in Genesis, we read that Adam and Eve went straight to fourth base: they questioned God when he said 'No' to eating the fruit on the tree. Adam and Eve questioned God's motive when he said that they would die if they ate the fruit; a mere snake helped them question this, and in conclusion to their questioning they ate the fruit, believing that God was lying. The outcome could have been very different if they had asked God for an explanation before eating the fruit.

Then there was Jonah, the famous whale guy, who questioned God when he was asked to go to Nineveh. Jonah questioned and complained to God because he did not understand.

The word of the Lord came to Jonah son of Amittai: 'Go to the great city of Nineveh and preach against it, because its wickedness has come up before me.' But Jonah ran away from the Lord and headed for Tarshish. He went down to Joppa, where he found a ship bound for that port. After paying the fare, he went aboard and sailed for Tarshish to flee from the Lord.

When God saw what [the people of Ninevah] did and how they turned from their evil ways, he had compassion and did not bring upon them the destruction he had threatened. But Jonah was greatly displeased and became angry. He prayed to the Lord, 'O Lord, is this not what I said when I was still at home? That is why I was so quick to flee to Tarshish. I knew that you are a gracious and compassionate God, slow to anger and abounding in love, a God who relents from sending calamity. Now, O Lord, take away my life, for it is better for me to die than to live.' (Jonah 1:1-3; 3:10-4:3)

The Bible is full of these people who questioned God, the religious books and religion itself. A few more are Job, Moses (Exodus 3:1-21), Peter (Matthew 15:12-19), Thomas (John 20: 26-31), Martha and even Jesus' own mother and brothers.

One of the well-to-do questioners in the Bible is a guy called Nicodemus (John 3); we will just call him Nick for our purposes. He was a great man; in fact, he was a leader or teacher at the Temple. He was a Pharisee. This man would have known the scriptures, he would have known his religion and he would have known the answers to any questions that anyone had about his religion. He would have worn his robes from the Temple, which at that time would have looked well cool; it would have been the equivalent to a businessman in London wearing a made-to-measure Armani suit and designer shoes. This man was no 'Sharon's Hair Bootee' at the corner of the street, but was a 'Toni and Guy' type of bloke: he looked the part, he worked for God at the Temple and he knew his religion inside out. But still, one night Nick found Jesus in secret and turned to him and said, 'You have done some amazing things, it blows my mind; you could only have done these things if God was truly with you.' (My rephrasing)

One thing that we know well about Jesus from the Bible is that he did his best to avoid compliments. We all love compliments but we never know what to do just after them. Well, Jesus avoided compliments with a fine art.

There are probably four things he could have done:

1. He could have said, 'Why, thank you, dear boy; nice robes.'

2. He could have sent the compliment right back to Nick, 'You too!'

3. He could have avoided it by pretending his Jerusalem hearing aid was not working.

4. Or he could have avoided the statement altogether and planned to confuse Nick – which is exactly what he did.

Jesus avoided the compliment from Nick and set out to give him a challenge. Jesus answered, 'I tell you the truth, no one can be in God's kingdom unless he is born again.'

What a jaw dropper! I can imagine poor old Nick standing there thinking, 'I only wanted to compliment him and now he has set me a puzzle.' Poor Nick turned to Jesus and said, 'Pardon?' Nick was confused about how someone could possibly be born again. He once again ventured to open his mouth. Nick quivered, 'How can a person who is now old enter back into his mother's body?'

Jesus once again opened his mouth, 'I tell you, unless one is born of the Spirit as well as the body he cannot enter into God's house.'

Nick, again with his head spinning, opened his confused mouth, 'WHAT?'

Jesus turned to Nick and asked, 'You are a very important man in Israel but you don't get this?'

Poor Nick, the man who knew his religion, was left confused by Jesus. Nick shows us that we can question our faith. He didn't go away and question what Jesus had said with others, who wouldn't understand what he had said either, but decided to stay with Jesus and try and understand and be challenged by him.

Jesus took Nick right out of his comfort zone; he challenged his understanding of religion and the scriptures that he followed. Jesus also challenged Nick about who he thought he was.

Nick didn't go away and talk about what Jesus had said with his other teacher friends: he wanted to understand Jesus and what he was saying. He could have run at any point and avoided the confrontation; he could have looked in his pocket sundial and said he had to go home, *Coronation Street* was on the telly. Nick was a teacher of the law, he was a very important man, but if he questioned Jesus and was challenged by him, the same can also apply to us. No matter who we are, no matter how long we have been Christians, or even if we are not Christians at all, we all have questions that need answering.

Spoon-fed

Many of us grow up in great little churches; with lively-ish worship, OK church leaders and growing youth groups, but 99 per cent of the time there is a problem with the way we approach our youth-group teaching. We don't question what we are taught in our groups; we take what is said and simply cram it into the God bit of our brains and accept it.

We can't just be spoon-fed our faith like babies; we need to question. Nick gives us permission to question; if a teacher of the law at the Temple questioned Jesus, then so can we. Nick was a fully-fledged teacher of God's law, but still did not know everything and still asked questions.

Our religion invites questions and it certainly does not condemn a lack of understanding. Jesus himself saw the confusion and questions from people 2000 years ago, and he also questioned God himself when on the cross. Jesus cried out, 'Why, Father?' (Mark 15:34)

But how do we question?

Nick not only allows us to question our faith, the Bible and the Church; he also shows us how to question.

Nick didn't question what Jesus was saying on his own, nor did he go and do it with people who would not understand, but he decided to question Jesus himself. This does sound a little unfair. Nick had Jesus to talk to but whom do we have? We can't talk to Jesus in the same way Nick did, since Jesus does not stand physically in front of us in the same way. But I do think we can learn from Nick using the same principles. Nick questioned with someone he could trust, with someone who could stretch him, with someone who could support him. These three principles are very important in our own questioning of our faith.

Three principles

Trust
We need to question our faith with someone we can trust, someone with whom we feel comfortable, and with someone who will allow us to say the wrong thing at times and still not judge us.

Stretch
We need to question with someone who will allow us to grow, stretch our understanding and not hold us back. This needs to be someone who enjoys learning too and someone who themselves is willing to be stretched.

Support
The third principle is support. We need to question with someone who will support us in our struggles and will help us to stay on the path, even though at times we feel like failing. This is someone who will commit to praying for you and being with you.

A cowboy or a professional?

Recently I had problems with my six-month-old washing machine and, as you can imagine, I was not impressed.

The front dial was ticking like an outraged egg timer; every time I tried to reset the dial it started again and went mental, ticking and clicking but still not working. After two hours of trying to fix it I decided to call a friend of mine to see what he thought I should do. His suggestion was to give the front dial a good whack! So I walked into the kitchen armed with a hammer and a shoe, and started hitting and beating it until it worked. But, of course, after half an hour of shouting and banging the washing machine was still not working.

If we have a computer problem we speak to a computer specialist; if we have a problem with an IKEA desk we speak to a handy man. As for my washing machine, I spoke to the people at the shop I bought it from and within a week it was fully recovered.

The same has to happen with our faith problems. We don't go speaking to a non-Christian about the Bible, they wouldn't have a clue. We need to speak to someone who understands the Bible. We need to question in a safe environment. Who better to question with but a specialist, a Christian?

Not yet

Nick was ready to ask his questions and hear Jesus' answers. Other people in the Bible weren't ready. For example, the 'Rich Young Man' (Mark 10:17-27) asked questions of Jesus but was not ready to hear his answer. When he asked what he needed to do to gain eternal life, Jesus told him to give up everything he had, from money to possessions. The rich young man went away from Jesus pretty upset. It's unbelievable the number of times we ask questions and think immediately afterwards, 'Did I really want to know that?'

I can think of a very good instance, which happened only the other day.

'How much do I have in my bank account?'

Before this question we happily assume there are sufficient funds to last an eternity, but once we have asked the cash machine, 'How much do I have?' a one-way path has been taken. The moment you press the button labelled 'Balance' you can no longer live in blissful ignorance.

'You have . . . £5.32 in your account.'

This is a question that many times we wish we had never asked. Or the times when we come home to find someone has tidied our room. Even though they think they do, they don't know where everything belongs or what is rubbish. 'Can you tell me where the phone number on my bedside table has gone?' We just know the response is going to be, 'Dunno, maybe I put it in with the rubbish.'

Sometimes we ask questions and we just aren't ready to hear the true answer. Too many times I have prayed and asked God for help in something, but never liked the answer he has given.

Sexy blue car

I was nine and at school, and we were asked to split into pairs for an afternoon of motorcar building. Each pair was given enough elastic, glue, balsa wood and paint to create and make our own car. At the end of the day we were to have a race to see whose car could go the furthest when we let them go on a very slight hill. We had only four hours to do this and I wanted to win. (A simple story with a sad ending – a warning if you can't see where this is going.)

So my partner and I set off designing our car, and it looked great. It was blue with a spoiler and huge wheels that we found on an old radio-controlled car. This car was our dream machine. We thought it looked excellent and we were keen to try it out. We took our car down to the playground, wound up the elastic fan at the back and, with our fingers crossed, let go. Unfortunately, the elastic-powered fan spun like mad, but the car didn't move.

At this point we went to seek Mr Birch's advice. We told him about our trial run and waited for his opinion. He stood up slowly, looked down on us and said, 'Boys, you need to lose the trendy exterior, build something simpler, something more aerodynamic.'

We were gutted. We didn't want to lose our cool-looking blue car with spoiler. We wanted to change the motor, but we didn't want a non-sexy looking car; we loved our good-looking car. We sat in the corner of the classroom knowing we were going to lose.

We weren't ready to hear Mr Birch tell us our car was rubbish; that wasn't the answer we wanted. And the same applies to God. Many times we come to him asking for an answer, but then are not happy with the answer he gives us.

If we ask something of God, he will answer – we know this because he has told us (Luke 11:10) – but we do need to put ourselves in a position to hear and be prepared to receive an answer that we may not like.

Nick put himself in a position to hear God but was not sure about the answer he received. The one thing I find most encouraging about good old Nick is the fact that even though he questioned Jesus about what it meant to be born again, and received an answer that he did not really like or understand, this did not stop him from following Jesus. We never really find out if Nick truly understood Jesus in the end, but even if he didn't, he still stuck by Jesus. We see Nick later in the Gospel of John defending Jesus in front of other Pharisees: 'Our law does not judge a man without hearing him and knowing what he has done' (John 7:50).

Even later we see that Nick is one of the guys who helped put Jesus' body in the tomb. 'Nicodemus, who earlier had come to Jesus at night, went with Joseph to carry the body' (John 19:39).

If Nick could question Jesus and still follow him, then surely we can too.

Going deeper

1. How often do you question your faith? And when you do question, to whom do you go to seek advice?

2. What are your top three questions? Are they your questions or are they questions you have heard other people ask?

3. Think about who you could chat to about your questions: are they wise? Will they help you find the answers? Will they give you the correct answers and not just the answers you want to hear?

4. Re-read the story of Nicodemus (John 3:1-21): what can you learn from him? In what way does he inspire you, and in what way does he help you in getting your questions answered?

5. Maybe write your questions down, pray over them, or give them to a friend to think about.

6. Because our real friends are concerned for us spiritually, they pray for us. In 1 Thessalonians 2:17-3:13 Paul prays for his friends; he asks that they will know God more and become more holy. How do you compare? Are you praying for your friends? Do you know what questions they have? Maybe you could pray together once a week/ month, and support each other?

QUESTION 2

How can a boring old book found in the strangest of places make any sense today?

I don't know about you but I hate reading. I have always had a problem with it and have found it a real struggle since I was tiny. When I was 11 my class at school was reading a book titled *The Iron Man* by a guy called Ted Hughes. It was a great book and it had us all gripped. Like all school projects, when you read a book you have all the lessons based upon it, and our project was to build the Iron Man.

Our Iron Man stood six feet tall in the corner of the classroom. Well, he did until the day one of the girls in my class knocked him over, and not only did she knock him over but she blamed me. By the time we rebuilt the Iron Man he only stood five feet tall, no longer a tall Iron Man glaring down on us from the corner of the classroom, but now more of an iron midget. And all this was blamed on me. As a punishment I was made to stand and read the entire book in front of the class. This moment of my life has moulded the rest of my reading life. I now hate reading and I loathe reading out loud.

We are living in a world where reading books is on the decrease but watching TV and DVDs is a growing pastime. So if we no longer read, what has the Bible got to say to us today?

Can we really trust the Bible?

It is very rare to find someone who says the Bible isn't an amazing book; most non-Christians would agree that it holds a lot of wise words. The sales of the Bible also indicate this as it has been the number one bestseller for years. Each year millions of Bibles are sold and most people would admit to having at least one Bible in their house; they may never read it but still it is there.

So, what is the Bible?

The Bible is a book made up of many books, 66 to be exact. There are 39 in the Old Testament and 27 in the New; it has history in its pages and also poetry, prophetic words, erotic literature (check out Song of Solomon) and suggestions on how to live. Forty authors, spanning more than a thousand years, wrote the Bible. If someone tried to write a book like it now using forty authors all writing on the same subject, I don't think that they would get the same harmony found in the Bible.

Saying that, millions of copies of newspapers are sold each day, but that doesn't mean they are telling the truth; sheer numbers don't prove anything. What about all the contradictions in the Bible, and all of Jesus' miracles, and do the people in the stories really exist? Perhaps the writers all sat down one day in a pub and thought they would write a jolly good book?

So, who wrote the Bible?

At school many young people used to think that the Bible was a book for extremely religious people and that its contents were written a long time after the events and were therefore incorrect. They even thought the fact that stories had been put together from what people had seen at the time made them flawed and even made up. An extremely large chunk of the Bible deals with these eyewitness accounts and first-hand information. If you were to write a book now about the Second World War, you would probably go and speak to someone who was around 60 years ago when the war was changing the world we now live in. You would probably find that some of the stories you were told would be slightly twisted and distorted over time; dates and places may be different and some of the information might be inconsistent. But as a researcher you would be able to cross-check the accounts to find out what exactly happened.

Chinese whispers

In our modern society, learning by passing information on by stories would not work very well. I was playing

Chinese whispers only recently. The sentence started as 'I saw a dog eating a can of cat food the other day' but by the time it had travelled around 25 young people it had become 'My girlfriend's a dog and she likes to eat cats'. In our society stories change and develop, making information passed in oral or spoken form very, very unstable. But 2000 years ago, when Jesus' followers were writing, it was a good form to use. Jews today still repeat their teachings and stories in just the same form as they did 2000 years ago. Telling each other stories was their form of radio and TV, and because of this tradition it was possible for the stories to travel for miles. But should a storyteller be creative with the truth (in other words, lie!) other eyewitnesses would keep the stories in check.

Do you remember what you were doing on 11 September 2001 when you first heard about the Twin Towers? I do. I can even remember where I was when I found out about Princess Diana's death, and many people remember where they were when President Kennedy was assassinated. We remember important dates and places. We sometimes forget where we were last week or even what we had for lunch, but we can remember the details of amazing events.

My chicken book

If I was to write a book titled 'The 17-foot chicken in Yorkshire' – the true story of a chicken that lived 20 years ago and killed several people – my sales may go through the roof but many of the readers would study it and know that this didn't happen. They would know Yorkshire and would not have heard any stories of 17-feet-tall chickens that lived in Yorkshire. People would know that I was lying and demand their money back. It was the same in Jesus' time, when the New Testament books were first starting to circulate; there would have been chaos if the stories were expanded, inaccurate and just simply made up. We would have known if the Gospel writers had been creative with the truth; people would have said something and put a stop to it. The reality is that the Bible is an accurate account of what happened, Jesus made an impact on the people he met, and people could not help talking about and sharing what they had seen.

Did you know there is more proof that Jesus existed than there is of Julius Caesar coming to Britain in 55 BC? There are only nine or ten manuscripts to support Julius Caesar's trip to Britain, and the earliest was written 900 years after the actual event. On the other hand, we have 2000 manuscripts of the gospels. We have in the Bible a very well-collected piece of history; the Bible is an authentic record of the events and times of Jesus, kept together over centuries with amazing accuracy.

What about all the contradictions?

While I was a student I worked every Saturday at a photography shop. Every time a new member of staff arrived they would ask me what I was studying and I would tell them the Bible. It was amazing that as soon as I said the Bible, the next question would be 'How can you believe in a book that is full of contradictions?' The best way to answer this question is to say 'What contradictions?' Most people who ask this question have actually not read it first-hand; they have heard a friend or a family member ask the same question, and, rather than look for them-selves, they choose just to accept what they are told. Most people – and not just non-Christians but many Christians too – get their knowledge of the Bible second-hand, and all they do is regurgitate the same inaccuracies and misconceptions.

I am a very bad speller, which comes from not being able to read very well: if I read more, then I may learn how to spell. Because of my lack of spelling ability, writing things like this is very slow and tedious. Someone who could spell must have created that dictionary! When you pick up a dictionary you have to start looking for the word you want, and not being able to spell it in the first place makes it impossible – it's like looking for a needle in a haystack. If I couldn't spell a word, then I would go and ask one of my friends. This was far quicker than looking in a dictionary, although often it was not very reliable. Like me and a dictionary, many people would rather get their knowledge second-hand than look for themselves.

I have read the Bible; I have even studied in detail many sections of it, and I can say that I don't think it does contradict itself. I do agree that many bits of it are hard to understand, many bits just don't seem to make sense on the first reading and even seem to go against other bits, but for me these contradictions are actually extremely minor contradictions and don't ever go against the main message of the Bible. The amazing thing was that the more I looked at the original language of the book and the world it was written in, and the more closely I looked and talked with my friends, the more I discovered that we can explain these contradictions with extremely reasonable answers.

Why aren't things like the big bang and evolution mentioned?

There are probably loads of questions you're going to have along the way about what the Bible does and doesn't mention. Unfortunately, this book just isn't big enough to do them justice – some need a book to themselves. We need to remember that the Bible was written by people who had no idea of things scientific, so you will not find words like 'atom', 'big bang' and 'evolution'. The writers talk about the 'whys' and not the 'hows'. Why was the world created? It was created because God is a creative and expressive being. How was it created? The Bible does not tell us how since at that time it was not thought to be important, because whatever way it was done, God did it.

Why don't the Gospels all tell the exact same story?

The four gospels are basically four different versions of the same story. Each is written by a different author, and set against a different cultural backdrop. Each of the gospels is created for a different audience, but all focus on the same amazing story.

Matthew was a Jew and his gospel is aimed at the Jewish reader. Matthew tries to show Jesus as their King. He quotes constantly from the Old Testament and argues that Jesus fulfils what was written there. Matthew leaves the reader with the only conclusion that Jesus was their Messiah. For Matthew it is very important to trace Jesus back to his ancestors to show that he comes from the line of David. The past is very important to the Jews so Matthew is careful to bring the past in.

Mark seeks to reach Roman readers by presenting Jesus as the perfect servant. Mark shows Jesus as ministering to the physical and spiritual needs of the human race. The Romans are very different to the Jews: they are constantly looking forward and are not interested in Jesus' past, so Mark sees it best not to add history to his gospel.

Luke tries to focus his writings on the Greek audience, depicting Jesus as the perfect man. Luke shows Jesus as coming to earth to seek and save the lost.

John is a bit different. He tries to broadcast the message to the entire human race. He decides to include seven miracles that Jesus did to show that he was the Son of God.

The four different writers were all writing for very different people, all adding and taking away what they saw as being appropriate for the culture they were addressing. The gospels don't contradict each other; they try to tell the story from different angles, allowing different sides of Jesus to come out.

Don't take my word on this: why not look for yourself? I believe that if you read the Bible with an open mind, then you will come to the same conclusion as me.

The great writers of the past

The writers of the Bible were not great poets or great writers like J. R. R. Tolkien or Charles Dickens, but they were ordinary men and women who could not magically make their words fit the twenty-first century in the same way as they fitted the time in which they were written. The Bible was written centuries ago half way across the world: this is why it talks about fishermen, tax collectors, slaves and emperors. Although it was written by ordinary people, that does not mean it is not God's words in the Bible. The Bible writers were writing with the power of the Holy Spirit: 'No prophecy ever comes from what a person wanted to say, but led by the Holy Spirit and spoken words from God' (2 Peter 1:21).

God used simple people to speak mighty words and he used them to put his inspired book together.

How is it relevant for today?

There are two things that we could do with the Bible: one is to rewrite it into modern language, using stories about skating and mini disc players; the other is to do what other Christians have chosen to do throughout the ages and that's to take the principles behind the words and then apply those to our new century.

I strongly believe that the Bible contains the answers for our living today. You see, although our chariots now have motors rather than horses and we wear jeans and suits rather than long flowing robes, humans today are pretty much the same as the people of 2000 years ago or even ancient times. We still all struggle with sin and suffering, along with raising families and trying to live day to day with integrity and meaning. Indeed, critics who call the Bible out of date do so not because it really has nothing to say to them but simply because the Bible disagrees with them. The Bible contains timeless suggestions for living our lives. Not just 'my truth' or 'your truth', but God's truth. The Bible's themes and suggestions for good living still apply for today. What about the themes of jealousy, murder, adultery, theft and not overdoing it (keep Sunday a relaxing day)?

Jealousy is still one of those things that we all

struggle with. We may not be jealous of our neighbour's donkey (although some people I know are a little bit weird like that), but we can be jealous of our friends mini disc player.

What about stress?

Our culture is full of stressed-out people living stress-filled lives, never having enough time for themselves or their families. What would happen if they kept Sunday as a non-work day? There would be more time to spend with those we love and consequently more families might stay together. God knew what he was saying when he wrote the commandments; they are timeless and only for our benefit, not his.

Because of these underlying principles the Bible will never be out of date; the world that it is written in might be, but the message within the world is timeless. *Oliver Twist* by Charles Dickens is a book set in Victorian times, but this does not make it out of date; many would agree that it is a timeless classic.

The Bible is only boring and out of date if you expect to pick it up and use it like a dictionary. You can't just turn to it when you need something. I don't deny that God can speak to us when we randomly open the Bible, but it isn't a magic book that we just open when we want. We need to become familiar with what it is saying, look at what Jesus said and did; we need to know the history that led up to Jesus and how this developed him; we need to know the world that it is set in. Only by doing this can we see how it is relevant for today in a way that no other book can be.

The writer of Psalm 119 knew this when he wrote, 'Your word is like a lamp for my feet and a light for my path' (Psalm 119:105).

Paul also understood what the scriptures were created for when he was writing to his mates in Rome: 'Everything that was written in the past was written to teach us. The Scriptures give us patience and encouragement so that we can have hope' (Romans 15:4).

The Bible is not a rulebook or a book to consult when everything is going wrong; we need to remember that the Bible is primarily God's 'rescue plan' for his people. The Bible has stood strong for centuries: philosophers, governments and even the Church have attacked it. The Bible has taken severe beatings over the last 2000 years but has been able to stand its ground. Try seeing the Bible not as the be-all-and-end-all of our faith but as a reminder of what God has done for his people; see it not as a rulebook but as a guide for the people he loves.

Going deeper

1. Read 2 Timothy 3:10-17. What do you think it means by 'God-breathed'? Do you treat the Bible like a problem page in a magazine only looking for answers, or like a person who serves God?

2. What is your image of the Bible? How does your image affect the way you read it? If you changed the way you saw the Bible, would it help the way you connected with it?

3. Which version of the Bible do you read? If it's not a youth-friendly version, why not try to find a more accessible version to read? There are loads of good translations around for young people. Also, why not try using some Bible study notes each day; they may help you get to some of the deeper issues.

4. If you find reading the Bible difficult, why not commit to reading a small section every day at the same time? It could be any time of the day; no one time is more holy than another.

5. Why not start reading the Bible from the gospels? They are much easier to read than the Old Testament. It is too easy to start in the Old Testament and get so bogged down with wars and death that you will never make it past the book of Kings.

6. Why not try praying just before reading the Bible? Ask God to help you understand it more through your reading. God can bring the Bible alive to us through the Holy Spirit, but we do have to invite him to help.

QUESTION 3
Is the line connected, because I can't hear anything?

I once knew of a young boy called Greg (name changed to protect the innocent) who was asked to say grace at the dinner table. He started his prayer well by thanking God for his mum, dad, brother, sister, grandma, grandpa, and all his aunts and uncles. Then Greg started to thank God for the food. He said thank you for the chicken, the mashed potato, the fruit, the pies, the cakes and even the strawberry dessert. Then he paused, and everyone waited . . . After a long silence, Greg looked up at his mum and asked, 'If I thank God for the broccoli, won't he know that I'm lying?'

In life we come across many weird and wonderful people. Some of these people are great fun and some are 100 per cent mad. But that does not stop us spending time with them. If you're anything like me, this means I do get some really wacky and weird conversations going. Once I sat on a train chatting to a nun for over an hour about how young people love reading *NME*. Other conversations have moved on to questions like 'Does God like Counting Crows?' 'Does God listen to music?' 'Does God own a music shop?' But then every once in a while I get some very challenging questions: 'Why doesn't God answer my prayers? Where is he?'

Sometimes with questions about prayer it would be easier just to say that he's gone on holiday, or opened a music shop in east London. Sometimes I go straight in with the Matthew 7:7 verse: 'Ask and God will give you'. Other times I bluntly ask, 'What have you been praying about?'

It is amazing the number of times the answer is 100 per cent honest but yet confusing and shows true frustration.

Chats about chatting to the big guy

Only the other week I had an interesting conversation with a young guy at a local youth event. After around five minutes the conversation went on to the topic of prayer. The boy was desperately praying for something and he felt that God was not letting him have what he wanted because God was a bully. Once I had calmed him down I tried to find out what he had been praying about. He then quite graphically told me how he had fallen for a girl at his school, and how he had asked her to go out with him, but she had only told him to 'go jump!' The poor boy was gutted; he really wanted this girl and would try to do anything to get her – even pray.

Another conversation with a girl at a local sixth form college was interesting. She told me how she too had been praying to God every night for weeks about something and he was not sorting it out. When I asked her what the problem was, it turned out that she was praying that God would get her a place at Manchester Uni to study medicine with her best friend.

Another young person told me that he had been praying that God would help him become a guitarist in a nu-metal band. But after a short time I worked out that the guy didn't play or even own a guitar.

It's amazing how many times when a conversation turns to prayer God is blamed for not answering the most amazing and weird prayers, like the young nu-metal rocker without any rock ability.

I would love to be God sitting in his engine room, reading all the prayers that he had received that day. I bet he laughs his socks off: God, can I have . . .? God, will you . . . ? God, he said . . . ? It makes me think: are some of our prayers worthy of God's ears or are they silly requests, like the ones a 2-year-old will ask in a sweet shop?

Asking like a child

The apostle Peter was very much like this, and would ask Jesus for the silliest of things. Peter was the ultimate child in a sweet shop. How can I say this of one of Jesus' disciples, the one whom Jesus appointed to start our Church? Well, I can, but only because he is a real fool sometimes.

On one occasion Jesus went with three of his disciples – Peter, James and John – to the top of a really high mountain (Matthew 17:1-8). Suddenly, with a flash of light Moses and Elijah, two of the most famous Jewish leaders from the Old Testament appeared, like a scene from a ninja movie. At this point all three of the disciples would have stepped back in awe and may even have had problems lifting their jaws off the ground. Now this is the bit where I really feel like slapping Peter. Jesus the Son of God is chatting to two dead guys from the Old Testament. What don't you do? I would certainly not have gone to chat to them – but Peter does. 'Jesus, it's great to see you chatting to your mates here – hope you're catching up with the gossip in heaven. I was just wondering if you wanted me to knock up a couple of tents for you and these guys so you can sleep here. We don't mind sitting here basking in your glory.'

Can you imagine Jesus' reaction? He didn't even have to think about it. Jesus turned to Peter and immediately answered, 'NO.'

Jesus knew that he still had work to do down the mountain with the people, and to stay on the mountain would waste precious time.

Peter isn't the only one to make silly requests; James and John do exactly the same thing. Just after the mountain incident Jesus and the disciples were denied a travel permit through a Samaritan village. This setback irritated James and John no end. Now remember who Jesus was and what he stood for – peace, love and life. What do you expect Jesus to do in this situation? No matter what you think he does, James and John's suggestion is far funnier. They are so angry at the situation they ask Jesus, a peaceful man, to burn the city with fireballs from heaven. Once again Jesus denied the disciples' request; in fact, Jesus rebuked them for asking it.

As the time approached for him to be taken up to heaven, Jesus resolutely set out for Jerusalem. And

QUESTION 3

he sent messengers on ahead, who went into a Samaritan village to get things ready for him; but the people there did not welcome him, because he was heading for Jerusalem. When the disciples James and John saw this, they asked, 'Lord, do you want us to call fire down from heaven to destroy them?' But Jesus turned and rebuked them, and they went to another village. (Luke 9:51-55)

If the disciples are capable of making weird and wonderful requests, then I'm quite sure we can do the same. Peter, James and John's requests were self-serving, materialistic, short-sighted and even immature. Could it be possible that we do the very same every day?

God loved the disciples far too much to grant their inappropriate requests, and the same goes for us. I don't believe we come to God with the intention of asking silly things of him and making inappropriate prayer requests. Often it isn't till way after an event that we can see our request is out of line.

It's like the story of me hitting my brother – at the time hitting him with a flight joystick seemed quite all right, normal even. But looking back I now know that hitting him didn't solve the problem, and in many ways made the situation worse as it caused him to fight later with larger and heavier gardening implements.

I think my most inappropriate prayer request was 'Please, God, change the other person, make them nice and not so rude to me' when actually it was me who needed to change.

I was talking to a young Christian youth worker called Gary about a year ago. He told me he was praying to God that he would turn a girl into a Christian, so he could go out with her. I had to ask, in the situation, did Gary's prayer request bring glory to God or did he only want something that would make him happy?

I think we need to think seriously about what we are praying for. Does our prayer

1. bring glory to God?
2. advance his kingdom?
3. help people?
4. help me to grow spiritually?

That all sounds well and good, but where does it leave us with unanswered prayers for situations of war, hunger and oppression? Surely prayers for starving children in war-stricken countries would bring glory to God and would advance his kingdom? And what about Christians who are sick, or those who are killed for their faith?

We need to remember that despite the victory God has achieved over Satan through Jesus' ministry, healings and the cross, everything is not yet submitted to God. The enemy is still active, although his years are counted and his end is sure, but in the meantime he still remains the prince of the world, and he opposes the ways of God. He causes much suffering and he often seems to have the upper hand. We have the assurance that all those very prayers which remain unanswered in this life will receive spectacular vindication in eternity.

He will wipe away every tear from their eyes. There will be no more death or mourning or crying or pain, for the old ways have passed. (Revelation 21:4)

We will look at the issue of why God allows suffering later in the book.

Fast food prayer

Many times we pray and pray like there is no tomorrow, and God just doesn't seem to hear our prayer. Where is God in this?

A lady came up to me the other day in church. She works with the 14–18s at her church. Although her group had been quite big it had dropped over the last year to four members. I offered to pray with her and hand it to God, in the hope that he would show her direction. But when I suggested this, she replied, 'I've already done that.' It turned out she had been praying for direction, but for only three days.

What are you like when it comes to Christmas? Do you love the season, the trees, cards and the food? What is the one thing you hate? Is it the fact that you have to wait until 25 December to open your presents? So many people go Christmas shopping with the family two months before the 25th, have seen what they are going to get and then really struggle to wait till that special day to open the wrapping.

Have you ever not wanted to wait two months for your Christmas presents? And then, when December has arrived, how often does your Advent calendar seem to hold back those last ten days to the 25th?

Have you ever known that you're going to get that new *Now* album or latest film on video for Christmas, and not been able to wait? Then, when your parents went out, you slowly climbed the ladder to get into the dark loft where the presents were wrapped ready for Christmas Day. And very slowly and carefully unwrapped the CDs till you found the one you were looking for and replaced it with another out of date CD and rewrapped the case.

Do you do that? You see I did. I climbed down from the loft and listened to the CD in my room without anyone knowing. The problem was this didn't just happen once but every year from the age of around 10.

We live in a society that wants everything now: we want fast food, fast computers, supermarkets with express checkouts, motorways with fast lanes, and film developing within the hour.

Have you ever been in a queue to have your photos developed? It's an amazing sight. People bring their holiday snaps for one-hour developing, leave them at 1.35pm and return at 2.05pm, only 30 minutes later, wanting them back. You stand in the queue watching as they argue with the salesperson. It doesn't matter how fast we can do something; we still want it twice as fast.

Tezzer

Too often we expect God to answer our prayers there and then. We want God to give the fast food response to our prayers, and we aren't prepared to wait. Imagine God answering our prayers in letterform. We send our request to God and he gets our reply ready. He then ties his response letter to the shell of his friendly tortoise, Tezzer. Tezzer is a wonderful guy but not all that fast, so Tezzer sets off climbing down from one cloud after another. Meanwhile, on earth, we are getting impatient with the delay of our divine reply, and eventually we get bored and move on to our next request. Too often we don't pray and wait long enough for God to reply; we just move on to our next fad.

I know that this story about Tezzer isn't overly scriptural – I mean, what would God do when Tezzer sleeps through winter? But I do believe it encourages us to persist in our prayers. If we do move on to other things, then surely it can't have been too drastic a prayer request in the first place. God sometimes makes us wait for a response to help us grow and mature in our faith, and to help us trust more in him. Sometimes God delays in order to test our faith, sometimes so that we can develop character qualities such as endurance, trust, patience or submission, and sometimes he waits so we can modify our requests.

God isn't a huge cosmic vending machine, like the ones at a local leisure centre where we put in our coins, tap in our request and it drops down in the tray below. God is a God who is watching over us and knows what we truly need. If I knew a vendor like God, then I hope it wouldn't give me a chocolate bar every time I asked for one but would sometimes give me a piece of fruit instead, knowing my waistline was already past bulging.

God said through his friend Isaiah, 'My thoughts are not your thoughts, neither are your ways my ways. As the heavens are higher than the earth, so are my ways higher than your ways and my thoughts than your thoughts' (Isaiah 55:8-9).

God sees things in grand widescreen multicolour

Have you ever tried to watch a game of snooker on a small four-inch black and white portable TV? I have seen people try. It's crazy! 'And there he goes to pot the grey ball with the white ball – ooh he accidentally knocked another grey ball.' It just can't work. Snooker needs to be seen in colour on a large screen, or else it just looks like dots hitting other blurred dots.

Or have you seen anyone trying to do 'Where's Wally?' when it's black and white and the size of a stamp?

We are like both these illustrations. We live life seeing only in black and white on a very small screen. Meanwhile, God is sitting in his comfy chair in heaven's engine room watching the world in 3D global technicolour with surround sound. God sees things on a much bigger scale. No wonder he knows what's best for us, he can see where we're going and what's in our future.

So where is God in our unanswered prayers?

Life is a little like a magic eye poster (if you've never seen one of these, then go to www.magiceye.com). From a distance it can look like chaos, colours blurring and swirling, making nothing but a colourful mess. It's only when we look carefully into the background of the picture that we can see an image. And like life, if we look carefully I believe we too can see an image in the background: the image of God.

Too often we look straight past what God is doing and don't even notice him. We need to take time to slow down and search for him in life; God shows himself when we spend time looking for him. He is there in unanswered prayer, perhaps not where we want to see him but in the background working quietly but surely.

Going deeper

1. What do you pray for in your regular prayers? Are they really worthy of God's ears or are they requests that are all about you?

2. Have a look at Nehemiah's prayer in Nehemiah chapter 1. The prayer is made up of worship, saying sorry, saying thank you and then finishes by asking for things. The areas are balanced with a bit from each. How much is this like your prayers? Which areas do you miss out the most? Are your prayers more like a long shopping list?

3. If you find it hard to know what to pray about or how to pray, why not ask a friend or someone you trust to pray with you a few times? Don't be scared to copy people's prayers when you first start; as long as they are aimed at God, he will not mind.

4. How long do you wait for a prayer to be answered? Why not keep a prayer journal to follow your prayers? Why not commit to praying for something or someone for a long period of time and wait to see how God answers your prayer?

5. Do you think that you may have some prayers answered in heaven – like it says in Revelation 21:4 – but not here on earth?

QUESTION 4
So if God is so loving, why does he allow suffering?

It seems so unfair when we hear of young people dying; we can't quite get our heads around why this should happen. Life at times just seems so unfair. We all know of people we love who have one thing after another that knocks them back and they never get back on their feet. But also we hear of world disasters that rock our feelings, our emotions and our sense of safety. I don't think many people will forget where they were when they first heard about the Twin Towers disaster in New York. 11 September 2001 will be a date that our generation will always remember. How can we not when images of the event were played over and over again in our own homes?

When we look at the natural and unnatural disasters over the last 100 years, including the First and Second World Wars, we all feel a deep sense of 'Why?' We can't justify the pain and struggles that go with the events. But the biggest question asked after all disastrous events is: how and why does God allow these events to happen, and why doesn't he just step in and stop them? Wouldn't it have been amazing if God had stepped in on 11 September and protected the two buildings by using a 'Mysterious God Protection Force Field', or decided not to allow the hijackers on the plane? Wouldn't everything have been OK?

We all struggle with this question. So does the Bible say anything about the world's suffering? I believe the answer is yes, but not directly. In the Bible we see a whole load of different reasons for the problem. When we look from Genesis to Revelation we see reasons why suffering happens, which we will look at now.

Lemmings

Lemmings was one of the biggest selling computer games of the early '90s. It was a cracker although very frustrating. The idea of the game was to try to get as many of the lemmings through a maze of some amazingly cruel and evil murdering devices. The devices used to kill the little green and blue lemmings were absolutely superb. One machine, my all-time favourite, made me cry with laughter. It would pick up one of the lemmings and fling it across the screen, making it land in what could only be described as a skinning machine. The lemming was then passed de-skinned and screaming across to another machine that would turn it into what looked like sausages.

Apart from the crazy killing spree, the idea was to try to get as many of the adorable little creatures to safety and back out of the level. The lemmings would enter through a trapdoor on the left of the screen and need to be guided across to their hut on the far right. It was the player's role to tell the lemmings what to do, and if the player didn't, then you could guarantee death within a few moments – if not by walking off a cliff, then by walking into the skinning machine. The lemmings were very silly, thick creatures and needed to be told exactly what to do. They were 100 per cent obedient to the player's demands and with the click of the mouse would dig, build, swing, block and even kill themselves for the player. The lemmings had no decision-making ability, and certainly could not rebel against the system.

A human lemming world

God could have created our world like the lemmings' world; he could have given himself the job of telling us what to do and when to do it. He could have decided not to give us free will, and made us, like the lemmings, totally obedient to the game player (God, in our case). God could have created a world of puppets that only he could tell what to do. But he didn't. He created us all with the ability of making our own decisions, living our life the way we want it. God created us with the opportunity for freedom, self-expression and questioning. God gave everything he created over to our control. Psalm 8:6 says, 'You put us in charge of everything you made, you put all things under our control.'

We aren't lemmings; we are living, breathing, thinking beings. God has put us in charge of his world; we are to care for and look after it for him. The problem is that it is often our bad choices that can lead to great suffering. It was my choice to hit my brother with the joystick and cause him suffering, the same way it is our choice to go to war and kill each other. Can God be blamed for our bad choices? He has given us tips for how to live life – 'Do not murder' – but we choose to do so anyway. Therefore, is it God's job to stop us, even though we have chosen free will and to live our lives as we want and not the way God has suggested? If I hadn't hit my brother, he wouldn't have been toothless and wouldn't have needed to spend the following two weeks searching through his poo to find his tooth, in the hope that the tooth fairy would leave him a pound.

There is something not quite right about our basic human nature, and the Bible calls this sin. Personally I hate the word sin; to me it conjures up images of Bible-waving preachers shouting, 'Repent! Repent of your sins, brothers and sisters, or you will rot in hell.' This for me and I think for many others, has given us a hatred of the word 'sin'; it has lost its sting and instead is a cheesy word with no meaning.

But what is sin?

This is a good question: what actually is sin? I want you to imagine what the world would have been like if there hadn't been the Fall talked about in Genesis. Humans would have been amazing, loving beings all created in the image of God; I'm talking about the way we act, speak and treat each other. We were all created with God's image in us, but because of the way we act and behave towards each other, and not accepting God, we have damaged this image of him inside us. Imagine every time we mistreat, joke about and mock our friends, we are spitting on the image of God inside us and distorting it. Most people think sin is having fun and not being able to see harm in it. Sin isn't just what we do; it is more about what we are like – we do what we do because of what we are like. It's all about how we treat God.

The problem is that we have distorted the picture of God inside us so much that many of us no longer know what is right or wrong, how to act and how to treat each other. Paul wrote to the Romans saying, 'So I have learned this rule: when I want to do good, evil is there with me. In my mind, I am happy with God's law. But I see another law working in my body, which causes war against the law that my mind accepts. That other law in my body is sin' (Romans 7:21-23).

Paul tells us it's our sinful nature within us that causes the suffering; we know what's right but still allow our urges to break through.

Chocolate

Do you like eating chocolate? Most people do and billions of pounds are spent on it each year. How often does lunchtime arrive and you think to yourself, 'I'll be good today; I will not eat any chocolate!' So you walk downstairs and make a nice big bowl of tomato soup with three or four slices of bread or a cheese and ham sandwich, sit down and enjoy it.

I wonder if the problem starts for people when they go out and walk past a corner shop and can't help themselves. They know they don't need chocolate after they've just eaten lunch and many times can't really afford to go splashing out on it every day. But the urge is too great. Does this sound familiar? I know I don't need to eat chocolate but my greedy nature inside me causes me to eat a king-size chocolate bar. That's the problem for all of us; we become greedy and want more of everything, more food, more money, more clothes and more of other people's 'stuff'. It's our sinful nature that is now a part of us that causes us to be weak against our worldly desires.

Changing the rules

Ice hockey is great fun. I find football boring, rugby's a thug's game and tennis a tad repetitive, but ice hockey is pure entertainment. The idea is to get the puck into the opposition's net, very much like hockey but on ice. From an outsider's viewpoint it may look like the game is very disorganised and that anything is allowed, but you would be very wrong. Like any sport, ice hockey is a rule-based game; break the rules and you will get sent off.

All sports have rules, and when the rules are broken madness breaks out. Imagine if in football a player was allowed to kick another player, or the goalie was allowed to run from one end of the pitch to the other holding the ball. The game would cease being fun and would cause people injury. And if an umpire changed the rules during a tennis match to suit what he wanted, the players would not know what they were doing, the line judges would be confused and the spectators would get bored very quickly.

The same is true with life. If one morning God decided that today everyone could fly or even swim like fish, the world would be thrown into turmoil. If God kept changing the rules of the universe every day, we would soon get confused and slightly miffed with him. And the same goes for the idea of God stopping two planes crashing into the World Trade Center. Why doesn't he change the way the world runs for one day? Why not put up his 'Mysterious God Protection Force Field'? Why not stop the planes? What we are really saying to God is 'Let us do what we want until it's something that the majority don't want', or even 'what I want'. What we are asking is silly. We often blame God for the suffering that humans have caused, and then we blame him for not stepping in when we want. We can't do what we want and still expect God to put things right. We can't pick and choose when God affects our lives; we need to allow God to affect our entire human lives all of the time.

I would hate it if my family and friends kept stepping into my life and telling me what to do all the time, but imagine how you would feel if someone you didn't like and didn't even want to know kept stepping into your life. The same goes with God. How would people who have ignored God feel if they kept finding him doing things to their lives? They would be miffed. But God does not act like an overprotective parent; he respects our choices to allow him or not allow him to change and affect our lives.

So where was God on 11 September? If he didn't put his 'Mysterious God Protection Force Field' over the Twin Towers, does that mean that he doesn't care? God did not cause 11 September, but he was there; he was there with the firefighters and rescue workers and the police; he was with the families and friends of those who died; he was there helping to relieve the pain. And we must never forget that on 11 September Jesus was there experiencing the pain and suffering of hanging on the cross, crying out, 'Father, forgive them.' Jesus was there, feeling our pain.

Not in God's blueprints

Suffering was not in God's blueprints. On the day of creation he didn't plan for suffering to be in the world, but he did plan to give humans the choice to live how they wanted. Through our wrong choice of living we have spoiled God's plan for the world and spoiled his creation (found in Genesis 3:6-7), and we have caused the world not to run in the way God intended. We have caused suffering to sneak into our lives because God's world has been taken over.

But why does God allow suffering and sin to enter the world? God loves every one of us so much, and I'm not talking about a love for the human race; I'm talking about a love that loves every single one of his children. The problem with love is that it can't be forced upon us. Have you ever fancied someone who isn't interested in you, or has someone who fancies you chased you but you were unable to reciprocate the affection? Love can't be forced on us and is only real if both partners choose it. God gave us all the choice and freedom to love him or not. Given this freedom, we have chosen to break God's recommendations for living, and the result of this has been our suffering. Life isn't purposeless and terrible, but this is what we have allowed to happen through being greedy and deceitful.

Can all suffering be because of us?

I don't think it is. Not all suffering can result from our sin; this isn't what the Bible tells us. One of my favourite programmes on TV is *One Foot in the Grave;* I love Victor Meldrew. You may think that this colourful and hilarious character was a creation of a TV comedy writer, but I don't think so. I believe that Victor Meldrew is a direct copy of the biblical character Job! Victor and Job have so much in common, to the extent that at one time I was thinking of rewriting the book of Job as a modern drama and asking Richard Wilson (aka Victor) to play the part.

What is the worst thing that has ever happened to you? Is it a bad hair day, or a huge spot on your chin the morning before a big date? Or is it turning up late to an exam or even not turning up at all? I find that the worst things always seem to happen to me on a Monday. Mondays are normally bad; it's the start of a new week and that means back to the grind. But the thing is I haven't met many people who can actually tell me that they had a worse day than Job. Job had worse than bad days.

Job was a great guy, well-liked, well-educated and very, very rich; but the best thing about Job was that he loved God and was committed to him. But one day, suddenly out of the blue, absolutely everything went wrong: he lost his entire family, including his wife and children, all his money was wiped out, and he became covered in huge ugly and very painful boils. This guy was having an 'I need a hug' day. Surely it couldn't get any worse, but it did. His friends arrived shouting and yelling that it was all his fault this had happened; he had obviously done something to cause this and upset God. The thing that I find hard about this story is that Job is a God-fearing man, who loves God and would do whatever he could to stick by God, but God allows Job to go through all this suffering even though he doesn't deserve it. It isn't until right at the end of the book of Job that he actually gets the privilege to speak to God. The thing is, God does not allow Job to know the reason why these things happened to him, but he simply shows Job his greatness and his justice. In the end, Job realises that what is important is not knowing the answer but knowing God. The thing that Job learns is that the more we know God, the more certain we can be that he will be fair in the end.

Suffering = punishment?

Many times Jesus expressed strong rejection of the automatic link made by many people between our sin and our suffering. On one occasion Jesus was walking along the road when he saw a man who had been blind from birth sitting on the roadside. It was at this point that his silly-question-asking disciples asked one of their silly questions: 'Teacher, whose sins caused this man to be born blind: is it his own or his parents'?' Jesus answered their question: 'It isn't this man's sin or his family's; this man was born blind so he could show God's power in him.'

Jesus points out that not all suffering is directly linked to someone's sin. He also points out that natural disasters are not necessarily punishment from God either. As Christians we need to be careful to look into our hearts when we are in deep suffering, but also remember that we need to be very careful about making judgements about why others are suffering.

The world is fallen too

For creation was subjected to frustration, not by its own choice, but by the will of the one who subjected it, in hope that the creation itself will be liberated from its bondage to decay . . . We all know that the whole creation has been groaning as in pains of childbirth right up to the present time . . . we groan inwardly as we wait eagerly for the adoption as sons and daughters, the redemption of our bodies. (Romans 8:20-23)

We need to remember that we live in a fallen world that is also groaning for the coming of Jesus. The world needs setting right in the same way that we all need setting right. All suffering is in some way linked to sin; it may not be my sin or your sin, or individual sin, but it is about living in a world that is not perfect. We need to remember that it might just be because we live in a broken world; since the world God created became malfunctioning, natural disasters could be the result of the confusion in the creation itself.

Going deeper

1. Read Psalm 8. Why do you think God left humans in charge of something so beautiful? Do you think this was a wise choice?

2. Have you ever caused someone suffering and not let them know that it was you? How much of other people's suffering could be caused by you?

3. What type of suffering have you experienced? Whom do you blame for this suffering? Do you blame God or the people around you?

4. What would you say to someone who had a relation that had died and they were blaming God for this loss? What could you do to help them?

5. In what ways can you see that God's creation is fallen?

6. Have you ever thought that your suffering is punishment from God? How does it make you feel to know that God does not punish us with suffering?

QUESTION 5
How can God really love me?

It's amazing the number of times that people of all ages ask the question, 'How can God really love me?' or 'How can God love me if my real dad doesn't?' It's hard to understand, if our friends and families don't appear to love us, how God can. Many of us come from families with loving parents but there are a growing number of people who don't actually feel that love.

The other question that is asked many times is 'How can God love me if I don't love myself?' All these are very good questions, and the desire to ask these questions demonstrates a deep searching for self-worth.

Newsflash

Most adults and some young people watch the TV news every night, but the thing about news is it's never good news. Recently, however, there was a story of a 13-year-old boy who spent $2 million on eBay from a school computer buying a full-size helicopter and jet using his mate's password. The boy's parents discovered the purchases the day the helicopter's owner called and asked how they intended to pay for it. The boy's family eventually had the purchases cancelled. The $1.1 million helicopter was a used military model, but the boy didn't make clear what he intended to do with it. This could only happen in America! I love funny news stories.

It's hard sometimes to work out what life is about when we watch horrific images on our TV screens about things that are happening in the world. Sometimes it leaves us scared but also wondering what this life is all about. People start to question the life that they lead themselves. They question what life is really worth and what they themselves are worth. It's amazing that many churches have seen Sunday attendance rise since the year 2000, not because of a sudden faith in God or great evangelistic events but because there is a real longing for self-worth. People are seeking to feel loved and cared for.

This question 'What am I worth?' is a good one to try and answer: what are we really worth?

Culturally

Culturally we are told that we are worth what we wear, what we eat, what we look like, what music we listen to and who we have on our arm. We are told that if we use this skincare lotion or the right perfume or even the right hair dye, then we are moving up in the world. We are told that if we live a particular way or in this particular house, then socially we are worth more than those living in less cared-for areas. We are told that designer clothes are better than straight-off-the-rail, and designer food is better than good old pub grub.

Scientifically

Scientifically we are only made up of a bunch of chemicals. If I chose to take a person and stuff him or her bit by bit into a human blender, and then spin them really fast in a huge centrifuge, this is what I would come up with:

- Enough fat to make seven bars of soap
- Enough lime to whitewash a hen house
- Enough sugar for seven cups of tea
- Enough iron to make a medium-sized nail
- Enough phosphorous to tip 2200 match heads
- Enough sulphur to rid a dog of fleas
- And enough water to fill six buckets

Scientifically that is what we are told we are made up of — just a bunch of chemicals — but that can't be all, can it?

Price tag

If I chose to take those bits of your body and sell them on the black market, how much do you think you would be worth? We are always being told that as human beings we are priceless, which is true; if someone dies, they are irreplaceable. But how much are we worth in pounds?

- £10
- £50
- £1000
- £50,000
- Or is it the priceless thing?

Well, I'm sad to say it's only £4.50. That's all you would be worth if you were sold on the black market. I could buy myself 20 humans for just under £100. Crazy, isn't it? Are we only worth what we have on our back? Are we only worth our flea-retarding capabilities? Are we only worth just under a fiver?

Shop owners think we are only worth the amount of money in our pockets. Socially, scientifically and the price tag on our head tells us that that is it. We have turned human life into nothing but the elements we are made up of, and our value into the money that we own. But is this right, or is there more to life than this?

Getting un-cool

Society tells us that we are only worth the stuff that we have, how good-looking we are, and how cool we look.

But the problem is all of this can fade. Our stuff goes out of date, our looks fade and our coolness melts away with age. Have you ever seen a cool dad? I mean, a *really* cool dad? I have seen interesting and funny dads, caring dads and loving dads, but I have yet to meet a cool dad. My dad was really cool in the '70s. I've seen pictures of him, and he looked like a member of Supergrass, with long hair, huge sideburns and large flares. My dad was an amazingly cool guy; I would love to have looked like him. Now, sadly, he looks like a member of the mafia with black suits, black sunglasses and going thin on the top. We can't stay cool for ever; we can try, but our tastes change and things move on.

The problem is that even our relationships can break down; relationships between friends, between parents and us, and between our parents themselves, can all fall apart.

All worldly things fade; they go out of date or are no longer wanted. The world is constantly changing, and we have to move with it. The problem is that as a society we don't have anything stable to hang on to. Or do we?

Where does God come into this?

Let's see what the Bible has to say about how God sees us and how he values us.

You know that in the past you were living in a worthless way, a way passed down from the people who lived before you. But you were saved from that useless life. You were bought, not with something that ruins like gold and silver, but with the precious blood of Christ, who was like a pure and perfect lamb. (1 Peter 1:18-19)

God sees us as worth more than gold and silver: worth the blood of his Son. My problem for years was that I could see how God loved the human race; he created it. But I could never see how he could love me; I was too small, too unimportant and inadequate for God possibly to even know me. The thing is, we are told over and over again in the Bible that we are worth a great deal in God's eyes.

For example, one day Jesus was doing his usual preaching in the streets and he'd worked up quite a good crowd. The tax collectors and the people that Luke calls sinners were crowding around Jesus in the street and really listening to him. Now the Pharisees were always complaining; Jesus could never do anything right. The Pharisees turned to Jesus and said, 'Look, this man welcomes sinners and even eats with them.' So what did Jesus do? He did the usual: he told a story to get them to think. This is what he said.

Suppose someone had 100 sheep and one of them gets a bit excited and decides to wander off as all young sheep do. The shepherd leaves the other 99 sheep and goes to search for the lost sheep, and he searches until he finds it. And when he does he calls his friends to celebrate the finding of the lost sheep. (Luke 15:4-6)

It wasn't often that Jesus explained one of his stories, but in this case he did. He said, 'I tell you the truth: there is more joy in heaven over one sinner who changes his heart and life, than over 99 good people who need not change' (verse 7).

Jesus was trying to say that God loves every one of his children, not just the good ones but also those who on many occasions have turned their back on him.

Too often in this world we have to earn love and respect. These things don't come for free; we have to prove our love and show commitment before we can be loved back. Well, this isn't what love is about.

What is love?

There are different types of love in the world and I have broken them down into four groups. You may not agree with me, but see what you think. I have listed them as natural love, affection, desire and self-giving.

Natural love is the love between a baby and its mum. It's the type of love that is first experienced at birth.

Then there is affection, which is the type of love between good old friends.

The third is desire, the lusting love, the love between two lovers, and is especially shown in sexual love. It is interesting how many times when the word love is mentioned people think of sexual love; for many young people sexual love is the only type of love to search for.

Finally, there is self-giving love, and for me this is the unique one. Self-giving love is only shown when someone gives everything they have to help someone else and never asks for anything in return. This is the type of love Jesus shows on the cross.

All these loves are in essence God-given, but because we live in a world that is off-balance, sin has distorted the first three.

This is why we see mothers and fathers not showing complete love to their children; or we see lovers beating each other up, or even sexual love being perverted. We live with a very twisted view of what love is; we don't receive it from others and we don't show it back. Love has become something linked to what we can gain; it no longer gives willingly but now asks for something in return.

I was asked the other week, 'How can God love me if my own father doesn't?' That type of question just makes me cry, because the twisted love that humans show hinders our view of God's love. Humans' love is no longer about each other but about 'me', but God's love is a love that is free-flowing and never-ending. God doesn't care what others think about us; he loves us no matter what. God's love is perfect. It doesn't come with any small print; there is nothing that we have to do to be loved. He loves us no matter what.

Loving the mess

So how can God love us if we don't love ourselves, or even if our own parents don't love us? The answer is simple. It's because of the fact that we don't know love that God loves. God's love stands in full contrast to the love that we know. While our love is manipulative, because it is largely self-centred and working in its own interests, God's love is 100 per cent unselfish.

God's love is not based on feelings or desires; it is not based on attraction; it doesn't seek to get its own way by tricking or psychological games. Rather, it flows from a heart of love and is directed to us to bless us and protect us. Its source is God and it's shown in Jesus Christ himself. God's love is not emotion but devotion and shown in his 100 per cent commitment to us, through his love on the cross.

We need to remember that God's love is not worked out by what we think about ourselves or by what others think, but just by the fact that God loves us as his children. God loves every single one of us as his child. God is a God of the small detail – after all, he created snow, didn't he? He loves us for all that we are and all that we can be. If you have never felt this love, why not read about it? It's there in the Bible – it's in the story of creation and the story of the cross – and if you can't see it, then try to feel God's hands around you right now. I promise you they are there!

Going deeper

1. How much do you feel worth? Why is this? What determines your worth?

2. Who are the people who tell you how great you are? (It could be your parents, friends or family or even your youth leaders.)

3. Have you ever felt what love is like really? Ask God to show you how much he loves you over the next few weeks.

4. Have you ever tried to manipulate someone to love or care for you? Or has someone tried to manipulate you? How does that make you feel now, looking back?

5. Read 1 Peter 1:18-19. How does it make you feel knowing that God loves you this much? Do you feel worth more, knowing that God loved you so much that he gave his Son for you?

6. Do you think it's possible for God to show you how much he loves you through other people? Why not choose one person and show God's love for them by helping them or supporting them?

QUESTION 6
Who really was the hippy in the sandals?

Was Jesus really who he clamed to be? Well, that is one of those questions that is a key girder to the whole Christian thing. If he wasn't, then we all might as well go pack our bags.

The facts

It is a fact that there was a man called Jesus who died 2000 years ago on a cross at the hands of the Roman Empire. It has been documented not just by Christian writers but also by non-Christians. There is sufficient evidence to show that there was a real man called Jesus of Nazareth who lived, breathed and walked 2000 years ago. This man single-handedly challenged the Jewish establishment and then, while in his 30s, was executed for doing so.

Jesus was not happy at just being a revolutionary in his hometown in Galilee where he was safe. He decided to travel to Jerusalem and confront face to face those who were actually responsible for the growing corruption of Judaism. Jesus didn't lead a revolution with weapons, but a revolution of peace. He healed the sick, made the blind see, and healed those who were lame.

This was until one night during the season of Passover, which Jesus and his friends were celebrating. Jesus turned to his friends and said, 'One of you is going to betray me', and he wasn't wrong. Later that night Judas betrayed Jesus in the Garden of Gethsemane with a kiss on his cheek. Jesus was arrested, questioned and labelled a blasphemer; he was then tortured and eventually condemned to death on the cross.

All of the above is widely accepted, but the question on many people's lips is 'Was he really dead when he left the cross?' If he wasn't, then the whole resurrection thing is blown to pieces.

At the end of the day was he really dead?

I really need to warn you this bit could get pretty graphic. (I once threw up after watching an early episode of *ER*, and this is far worse!)

It starts with Jesus being whipped. The whip used would have had pieces of sharp bone attached to strips of leather, which would cut his flesh severely. This is where it starts getting gruesome. The whip would have shredded Jesus' back so badly that part of his spine could have been showing in the deep lacerations. It is a fact that many would not have made it past this stage; the whipping would have been so bad that they would have died there and then, and never made it to the cross.

At this point Jesus' heart would have been racing, trying to make up for the loss of blood. He would have had dangerously low blood pressure, causing him to faint or even collapse. Jesus would have been extremely thirsty as his body would have been craving fluid due to blood loss. We can see this in the gospel of Matthew: 'As they were coming out, they met a man named Simon and they forced him to carry the cross' (Matthew 27:32). Jesus was so tired, faint and near to the point of collapse that he couldn't carry his cross, so they had to get someone else to carry it for him.

The Crucifixion

Did Jesus truly die on the cross? Well, tell me what you think after this. The Romans would have laid Jesus down on the ground, stretching his arms across the horizontal beam. Then they would have driven huge nails, around six inches long, into his wrists. This nail would have gone straight through the largest nerve going to Jesus' hand; the nail would have crushed the nerve producing intense pain. Imagine the pain you get when you hit your funny bone – this pain would have been constant. It would be as if someone had taken a pair of pliers and squeezed his nerve until they crushed it.

The pain that is experienced during crucifixion is so bad they had to create a new word to describe it: this word is 'excruciating', which means literally 'out of the cross'.

Jesus would have been raised up on to the cross-bar and attached to the vertical beam. The nerves in his feet would have been crushed in the same way as those in his wrists as the nails were driven through them. As he hung there, his arms would have been dislocated from his shoulders.

The death

Crucifixion is a painful, slow death, but death does not come from being on the cross but from the fact that the person cannot breathe. Since both of Jesus' hands and feet were nailed to the cross, breathing was unbearably painful. Jesus would have had to push up on his feet so that the tension in the feet was alleviated. In doing this, the nails in both his feet would tear the skin and muscle till it locked into the bone. Now Jesus would have been able to breathe in, would then have relaxed and breathed out, but then almost immediately would have needed to take another breath, which would mean raising himself back up again. Remember all this would have also caused the wounds on his back to rub on the wood. This pain would go on till he was too tired to breathe any more.

Can you cope with any more? Jesus' breathing would have slowed until he went into respiratory acidosis. 'What is this?' you may ask. Basically, the carbon dioxide in Jesus' body would have caused his blood to become acidic and this would lead to a very irregular heartbeat. This would have been the point at which Jesus would have known that his moment of death from cardiac arrest was approaching.

You can ask any doctor. In fact, next time you go to see your doctor, read out the account of Jesus' death to him/her from the Bible and ask them if they think he could have lived through the entire trauma. There is certainly no doubt among doctors or medical experts: they all agree when they read the Bible's account of Jesus' death that he was dead.

Is there any way that Jesus could have done a runner?

Could Jesus have left the cross alive? I don't know what you think, but my reaction is 'absolutely not'. I have heard so many times the theory that Jesus merely fainted on the cross and regained consciousness in the tomb, unwrapped his mummy cloths, then rolled the huge rock away from the door, and ran quietly past the Roman guards. Even if he hadn't died on the cross, think about the pain that he would have been in: no skin on his back, a huge hole in his hands and feet, a large cut in his side and cuts on his head!

I don't know about you but I can't cope with pain. I was on my bike once when a bully from school pushed me off it; he pushed me off using a football in a plastic bag – nice! I fell off the bike cutting both arms and knees and, boy, did it hurt. I then had to walk home pushing my bike, limping and wincing at the pain with blood dripping down my arm. Now if that hurt for me, then think about how much pain Jesus would have been in; it would have taken weeks if not months for him to recover.

A final nail in the coffin of the 'Jesus was alive on the cross' theory is this: that if by some miraculous Impossible Mission-style acrobatics, Jesus quietly flew, walked or even swung past all of these hurdles and made it out of a grave, many questions are still not answered. I mean, how did he walk with huge nail holes in his feet? Have you ever had a splinter? You can't move with a splinter in your foot, and you certainly can't walk with a nail hole in it. Remember that he was seen on a Sunday stroll on the Emmaus road – that's got to have hurt. What about his arms and shoulders out of joint? They don't just pop back in. Jesus was seen three days after his crucifixion, walking and talking: he could not have done this fresh off the cross.

And, finally, the Romans were expert at crucifixions; they had done loads and knew the difference between a live person and a dead one. When they stabbed him in the side, they were checking to see if he was dead. When a person died their blood separated into water and blood. There is no way that the Roman guards would have let him off the cross if he was still alive, especially considering that he was thought to be a troublemaker. He was definitely and completely dead.

I'll be back

If Jesus died on the cross, as the facts tell us, this does not prove that he rose again. We do know that his body disappeared and that there was a huge Roman cover-up, MIB-style. But the fact is the crucifixion was true; it has been documented. Jesus, a rebel from Galilee, was crucified. The hard bit is the resurrection. What happened to the body? Did the disciples steal it? Or did the women forget which tomb it was in?

I see that there are three possibilities . . .

The women and disciples lost the tomb

The women, in such stressful circumstances, may have forgotten which tomb Jesus was in, or the disciples, in a brief brainstorm, could have lost the directions, but there was no way that the Romans (creators of straight roads and amphitheatres) could have forgotten where it was. They had men guarding Jesus and these guys were good: nothing would have got past them.

The Christians stole it

If the Christians had walked off with the body, they could have continued the fame of Jesus. 'He's alive, we've seen him!' Yes, they had seen Jesus: he had been wrapped in cloth and was smelling in someone's fridge – maybe Peter's with all the fresh fish. What doesn't add up is this: what was the point following a man to your own death if he himself was dead? Would most of us follow directions to our death from a living mad man, let alone a dead one?

Tradition says that Peter was crucified upside down, Stephen was stoned and John was hurled into a large pot of boiling oil – all for talking about the risen Jesus. What would they have gained? What was the point?

The non-Christians stole it

It could be that the non-Christians/Romans walked off with the body. Although if you played a football game and you won, wouldn't you want to boast about it? If they had stolen the body and the Christians were shouting that they had won, wouldn't they put an end to the madness and show everyone Jesus' body? The Romans wanted to silence the Christians; what better way than to wave the dead body around?

The problem was the Romans couldn't cover up the fact that Jesus' body had gone when so many people had seen him during the weeks after his death.

Going deeper

1. Look on the Internet or at your local library for things that you can find about Jesus. Try to find out historical information documented by people other than Christians.

2. Have a look for information about crucifixion.

3. Read the account of Jesus' death in Luke chapters 23-24. Take your time reading it. Why not put on some mellow music and spend some time imagining what it must have looked, smelt and sounded like? Try and imagine being there, seeing it first-hand.

4. If you have any doubts about Jesus and his death, why not talk them through with a mature Christian? Question what they believe and ask them what bits they find hard to get their head around.

5. Try watching a clip from *Jesus of Nazareth*. See how they document Jesus' death and resurrection. Do you think this is how it was told in the Bible? How is it the same and how is it different?

QUESTION 7
Jesus + death = freedom. How does that work, then?

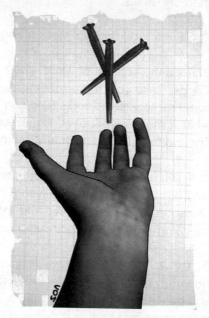

Get this. We are told that 2000 years ago a hippy with a long white dress and Nike Air Jerusalem sandals walked around a very sandy, hot country. We are told that he was a good man, a holy man and that this man could do some amazing stuff – I mean, have you ever seen a guy walk on water or heal a leper? We are even told that he was the Son of God. Now, if this is true, which I believe it is, how can this man dying 2000 years ago mean that my sin is forgiven? It's like saying that a guy dying in Australia could forgive a murderer in prison in the UK. If one day I walked into the Old Bailey and trotted up to the judge in an evil murder case and asked if I could serve the sentence instead of the real killer, the judge would think I was mad. He probably wouldn't let me go to prison and serve the life sentence; more likely he'd order me to be sent to a mental hospital.

Another way of looking at it is to imagine that a close friend copied your exact essay, right down to the dots on the I's and the crosses on the T's. They get caught and, to save them from being kicked out of school for cheating, you decide that you want to take their punishment for them, the consequence being that you will be booted out of school. It just doesn't make any sense; the teacher would laugh and send you back to your class.

So how and why can Jesus' death mean that every-thing I have done to people – all my words of abuse, all the times that I did what I wanted and lived how I wanted – can be forgiven because of the cross? It just doesn't make any sense. Or does it?

Sacrifice

We need to start at the beginning; to make a little more sense of it we need go way back. We, with our twenty-first-century ways, have lost any real sense of what sacrifice is. Now we see it as an occult practice, but only 2000 years ago it was a way of life.

Ouch, that must hurt!

In the Old Testament, sacrifice was a universal way of life, although the item being sacrificed and the way it was done would have varied. In Israel there were sacrifices of wine, but the most important was the animal. This is what would have happened. Again, if you're squeamish, look away now.

Imagine if a Jew – let's call him Mr Very Bad Sinner, or Brian for short – had committed a series of sins during the year – maybe theft, murder and adultery. In God's eyes he would be stained by these sins and would have to sort them out. So Brian would bring an animal to the altar; let's say it was a cow called Daisy. Brian would lay his hands on the animal and confess his sins on to the cow. Daisy would now be the bearer of the sin, poor old Daisy. Brian would kill Daisy by slitting her throat (I told you to look away) and the dead cow would be burnt as an offering to God.

But why was poor Daisy offered?

Why should our old pal Daisy have to suffer? This is a good question. One reason why Daisy had to die was because it was about offering something to God that was valuable and had meaning to us. These days it might be your PS2, mountain bike or CD collection. The other reason is related to what we already know about how sin causes a blockage between us and God and how humans walk away from God's ways. God could have done two things: he could have said, 'Well, forget them; I'll leave them to it' or he could have said, 'They have done everything I didn't want them to, they have walked all over me and my creation; but I still love them.'

Thank God that he decided to go the second way: he decided to allow humans to put things right; he gave them a way of being set free from their sin. 'Once a year Aaron must make the altar ready for sacrifice to God by putting blood on its corners, the blood of an animal offered to remove sins' (Exodus 30:10). God gave sacrifice as a way to remove the sins. We are told in the New Testament that 'the cost of sinning is death' (Romans 6:23).

If we sin, the only way to put this right is death. God gave the Israelites a way to pay for sin without having to kill them. But they could not kill any animal; there were very strict rules about what could be given as a sacrifice. The animal had to be clean and 100 per cent pure and perfect. Wild animals were seen as already God's and couldn't be given to him in a sacrifice.

God said that something had to die. In God's eyes Brian's life was stained by the life that he had led. So God gave Brian a way of transferring his stain to a pure animal, and in this substitution Brian was given the pure life of the animal. Sounds very gruesome, but it worked – until the time of God's new way.

Sacrifice in the new way

This is where Jesus came into it. Jesus the once-and-forever sacrifice – no more killing and burning poor old Daisy. God decided to be the ultimate sacrifice; God himself became the rescue plan, the ultimate superhero.

Jesus hanging on the cross was a once-and-forever act. So how can one man die for us all and forgive our sins? It's hard to get our heads around, but imagine God the creator not wanting to leave things as they were, God not wanting the devil to have hold on us, God longing to put things right and allow us to live a life with him again. So what does he do? He takes on the devil in the ultimate wrestling match and fights for everyone. God dies for everyone's sacrifice.

The Mexican bus driver

I was on the CNN web page when I came across one of the saddest stories I have every heard. It was one of those real-life stories that makes life feel so fragile and makes your heart miss not just one but several beats. I have not been able to find out if it really was a true story or not, but it gets the point across.

A man called Cibeles worked as a school bus driver. He drove children to and from their local school, which was situated on the outskirts of a large Mexican town. Cibeles was described as the best school bus driver the children had ever had: he was kind, caring and a very protective driver. Cibeles loved his job and the children in his care, although the children he drove were all very disobedient and rude. Each day the children would call Cibeles names, throw things at him and punch him when leaving the bus; they were very badly-behaved children.

One summer's day in July 2001 Cibeles was driving around 40 children home in his over-crowded bus. The children were screaming and yelling and throwing things down the bus at Cibeles. Everything was just as normal – busy roads, noisy children and cramped streets. Cibeles turned the bus left on to a very tight street with parked cars on both sides of the street but the worst thing about this street was the steep hill – this was one of the steepest streets in town. Cibeles suddenly saw a child run into the road. Cibeles knew straightaway that because of the overfull bus, the steep hill and the distance from the child he would not be able to stop in time.

He had to make a choice: should he swerve to avoid the child but drive into a street full of cars, probably killing all the children on the bus, or should he brake and kill the child? The choice was to kill one child in the road or a busload of children. What would you have done? It's a hard choice. What made the choice even harder was that Cibeles recognised the child on the road as his only son, aged 13.

Should he kill his own son to save the badly-behaved children who gave him grief every single day, or save his son? With only seconds to act, Cibeles drove directly at his son, killing him instantly.

Does this story ring any bells? God could have allowed every human to die but chose instead to kill his Son. Cibeles, too, chose to kill his son to save 40 children who didn't even respect him. Cibeles and God were both treated with contempt. Cibeles' child and God's Son, again both treated the same, were sacrificed for others' lives.

The loss of sacrifice

The problem is that as a society we have lost a sense of sacrifice for the people we know and certainly for those we don't know. As a nation we have lost the sacrifice of giving money to charities, giving time to help the community, and we have lost the sacrifice for those we call family.

The other week at my church youth group we were looking at friendship and how we treat friends, and one of the conclusions we came up with was that in real love and real friendship there has to be an element of sacrifice. We found this in John 15:13: 'No greater love is there than a friend that sacrifices his life for his friends.'

I decided to try this out, so I turned to a group of girls in the corner and asked Clare if she would do anything for Sarah; the answer, as I knew it would be, was 'Yes'. So I then asked Sarah the same question and the answer was again 'Yes'. I asked Clare if she would give her last Rolo to Sarah, and the answer was 'Yes'. We all knew that they were best friends – they were inseparable, always wore the same clothes and listened to the same music. So I turned to ask Sarah the deadly question, 'Would you give up your boyfriend if Clare liked him more than you did?' Her face went white. Could Sarah make that sacrifice for her friend? The answer came: a sorry 'No'.

We have all lost a sense of sacrificial love: we would never dream of letting ourselves go in someone else's place; we are constantly thinking about what we can gain, what we can achieve and how we can make ourselves look good in others' eyes.

Why did God let his Son die for us? Well, it's because he loves us. How can Jesus dying help us to be clean? Well, it's because sin equals death and someone had to pay the price.

Imagine going to a supermarket and filling your trolley with everything you wanted and then getting to the checkout and not being able to pay the bill. And then from behind you, a hand appears with a debit card that will pay for any amount. It's the same: we have run up a sin bill, we are unable to pay the charge and God holds the card to wipe away the bill and pay the price.

I want to end this chapter with a story I heard many years ago. I still don't know who the true author is – I've heard it told many times in many different ways – so thank you, Mr Unknown Author, I would love to meet you some day and say thanks for this, I think it's great!

The room

In that place between wakefulness and dreams, I found myself in a room which had walls covered with small index card boxes.

I walked to a wall of boxes. The first to catch my eye was the one that read 'People I have liked'. I opened it and began flipping through the cards. I quickly shut it, shocked to realise that I recognised the names written on each one. Then, without being told, I knew exactly where I was. This lifeless room with its small boxes was a crude catalogue system for my life. Here were written the actions of my every moment, big and small, in detail.

Some brought joy and sweet memories; others a sense of shame and regret so intense that I would look over my shoulder to see whether anyone was watching. A box named 'Friends' was next to one marked 'Friends I have betrayed'. The titles ranged from the mundane to the outright weird: 'Books I have read', 'Lies I have told', 'Comfort I have given', and 'Jokes I have laughed at'. Some were almost hilarious in their exactness: 'Things I have muttered under my breath at my parents'. I never ceased to be surprised by the contents. Often there were many more cards than I expected; sometimes fewer than I hoped.

Each one was in my own handwriting, each with my signature. When I pulled out the box marked 'Songs I have listened to', I realised that the boxes grew to hold all their contents. The cards were packed tightly. When I came to a box marked 'Lustful thoughts', I felt a chill run through my body. I pulled the box out only an inch, not willing to test its size, and drew out a card. I shuddered at its detailed content. I felt sick to think that such a moment had been recorded.

Then I saw it; the title was 'People I have shared the gospel with'. I pulled on its handle and a small box, not more than three inches long, fell into my hand. I could count the cards it contained on the fingers of one hand. And then the tears came. I began to weep; sobs so deep that the hurt in my stomach threw me. I fell on my knees and cried. I cried from the overwhelming shame of it all. No one must ever know of this room. I must lock it up and hide the key.

But then as I wiped away my tears, I saw him. No, please not him. Oh, anyone but him. I watched helplessly as he began to open the boxes and read the cards. I couldn't bear to watch his response. And in the moments I could bring myself to look at his face, I saw a sorrow deeper then my own. He seemed intuitively to go to the worst boxes. Why did he have to read every one? Finally he turned and looked at me from across the room. I dropped my head, covered my face with my hands and began to cry again. He took out a box and, one by one, began to sign his name over mine on each card.

'No!' I shouted, rushing to him. All I could find to say was 'No, no', as I pulled the cards from him. His name shouldn't be on these cards. But there it was, written in red so rich, so dark and so alive. The name of Jesus of Nazareth covered mine. I don't know how he did it so quickly, but the next instant, it seemed, I heard him; he placed his hand on my shoulder and said, 'It is finished.'

Going deeper

1. Have you ever done something to save someone else's skin? Or have you ever given up something to help someone less fortunate than you?

2. Read Romans 6:23 (The cost of sinning is death). Do you think that this statement is over the top? What do you think is the cost of sinning?

3. A guy called Irv Kupcinet once said, 'What can we say about a society that says God is dead and Elvis alive?' In your opinion, what is it that people see in Elvis and the belief that he is still alive, but don't see in Jesus?

4. What would you say are your top five sins? How would it make you feel if close friends knew what they were? How does sinning make you feel? How often do you think that you go against God's ways to follow your own ways?

5. Do you think that what Cibeles the Mexican bus driver did to save the busload of children was a wise choice? What would you have done?

6. In 'The room' story, was there anything that made you feel uncomfortable? Was it because of what it was saying, the imagery used, or the fact that it made you think of the contents of your drawers?

QUESTION 8
Does the Holy Spirit have legs?

The Holy Spirit is a matter of controversy right across the Church.

It's not too difficult to understand that God the Father created everything, using a huge science kit called 'Whiz Bang: create your own universe in three easy stages', which he ordered on the net from www.creation-r-us.co.uk. You can image him reading the instructions: 'Store your universe safely, in a closed box, somewhere cool and dry, out of the reach of children and animals, until the time it is needed. Never put a universe in your pocket. Make sure all pets are inside. After the creation, use tongs or gloves to collect spent universe parts. Next morning, check again and remove universe debris. Just add water.' He lit the fuse like a giant firework and stood well back waiting for a large explosion.

Again, Jesus isn't that difficult. He's God in human form, living on earth, moving into the neighbourhood, sharing his Father's love, and then ultimately dying for everyone's sins. (If you're reading this and thinking, 'Hey, I don't get Jesus', then why not skip back to previous sections?)

The thing is, we can see the Father's creation each day, and we have historical and biblical proof that Jesus lived – we can even have a relationship with him if we like. But it's hard to understand the other part of the Trinity.

Who is the other guy?

Depending on what type of Bible you read or what kind of church you go to, you may know him as God's Spirit, the Holy Spirit or the Holy Ghost. The problem is this creates images of something quite terrifying. A ghost that floats in mid-air, able to go through walls, and something you have no control over and no relationship with.

To put your mind at rest, the Holy Spirit is not a ghost or anything scary, but a person who thinks, acts and directs.

So what does the old book say about him?

He thinks and directs: 'It seemed good to the Holy Spirit and to us not to burden you with anything beyond the following requirements' (Acts 15:28).

He speaks to us: 'Peter stood and said, "Brothers, the Scripture had to be fulfilled which the Holy Spirit spoke long ago through the mouth of David concerning Judas, who served as guide for those who arrested Jesus"' (Acts 1:16).

He takes us on a journey and leads us: 'Because those who are led by the Spirit of God are sons of God' (Romans 8:14).

He was fully a part of the creation process; he was the one who breathed life into all of us: 'In the beginning God created the heavens and the earth. Now the earth was formless and empty, darkness was over the surface of the deep, and the Spirit of God was hovering over the waters' (Genesis 1:1-2).

He is described as the Spirit of Christ: 'You, however, are controlled not by the sinful nature but by the Spirit, if the Spirit of God lives in you. And if anyone does not have the Spirit of Christ, he does not belong to Christ. (Romans 8:9).

The Bible speaks heavily of the Holy Spirit; he is described in many ways and as having many attributes. He was promised by the Father and by Jesus; he is called the counsellor, the wind, the fire and many other names. In the Old Testament the Holy Spirit gave people great power, the ability to lead, to perform great acts of strength in battle and even prophesy. (God also promised that when the right time came the Holy Spirit would come in a radically new and powerful way.) In the Old Testament the Holy Spirit would only be with some people; these tended to be great kings or amazing prophets.

But God said that the Holy Spirit would come and be with everyone all the time: 'I will give you a new heart and put a new spirit in you; I will remove from you your heart of stone and give you a heart of flesh. And I will put my Spirit in you and move you to follow my decrees and be careful to keep my laws' (Ezekiel 36:26-27).

The busy time

Until Jesus' coming the Holy Spirit had had an easy time of it, spending time with godly men and royalty. But when Jesus came on the scene things started to heat up, and the Holy Spirit had to get himself into gear.

We see the Holy Spirit making Mary pregnant, appearing in the form of a dove at Jesus' baptism and giving Jesus his almighty power. But it's not until after Jesus' death and his coming back to life that the Holy Spirit really started to work.

Imagine: Jesus died, came back to life, spent some time chatting to his mates, did some more healing and then after a few weeks made his way back to his Father in heaven. Jesus didn't just go and leave it at that: he told the disciples to go out and make new Christians all over the world, and to wait for the Spirit.

The day of Pentecost came. The disciples were sitting in a locked room when suddenly a gust of wind blew around. You can imagine there were probably many scared faces but also a few one-liners going around the room: 'Hey, Peter, no more beans for you!' and 'No one strike a match!'

Then, as the heckling passed, the Holy Spirit came in a completely new way. The disciples had flames coming from their heads. (I always wanted to know if God used safety matches for this event or if he had a fire extinguisher to hand just on the off-chance something went wrong, like Tim's tunic lighting up or John's toupee singeing.) The disciples found themselves speaking in new languages, having the confidence to talk about Jesus and the power to heal. They had a new breath of life blown into them and the power to live for God.

So what does he do for us?

It's great to hear what the Holy Spirit has done for some of the Bible's great leaders. But what does he do now and what does he do for us?

For a moment we need to go back to Nick in Question 1. Nick, the great church leader, came and spoke to Jesus and asked him how you could be born again. Jesus answered, 'I tell you the truth, no one can enter the kingdom of God unless he is born of water and the Spirit. Flesh gives birth to flesh, but the Spirit gives birth to spirit. You should not be surprised at my saying, "You must be born again"' (John 3:5-7).

The Holy Spirit comes to give us a new life – a new birth into God's family. Think about it. Your mum physically brings you into this world but the Holy Spirit gives us a new birth into God's world. It is only by being born with God's Spirit that we can really get into God's world; no words, no action, not even money can get you there, only the Holy Spirit. This does not mean that you have to be physically reborn – that would be impossible and very painful – but filled with God's Spirit and changed to become more like him.

The Holy Spirit also helps us to read the Bible and pray: 'I keep asking that the God of our Lord Jesus Christ, the glorious Father, may give you the Spirit of wisdom and revelation, so that you may know him better' (Ephesians 1:17).

He helps us to open our eyes to see new things in the Bible; he helps us to understand more and more of God's ways and not our ways. He gives us wisdom to understand what God is doing and wisdom to make decisions. The Holy Spirit also reveals bits of himself to us. God is passionate about the poor and lonely which means that when we pray and speak to God we might also become passionate about injustices in the world. The by-product of this is it gives us more to pray about. God wants us to be praying and learning more about him daily, and this is where the Holy Spirit comes in. God gave us the Spirit to help us become more like him, to make things clear and to give us the things we need to share our findings.

'Now the Lord is the Spirit, and where the Spirit of the Lord is, there is freedom. And we, who with unveiled faces all reflect the Lord's glory, are being transformed into his likeness with ever-increasing glory, which comes from the Lord, who is the Spirit' (2 Corinthians 3:17-18).

Silly games

Every Christian has the Holy Spirit living in them. Imagine your life is like a large living room. Windows, chairs, tables, lights, bookcases and lots of other clutter. The Holy Spirit can sit on the soft sofa in the middle of the room and be a part of everything going on. Or he can sit in the corner behind the bookcase and never be used or spoken to.

Have you ever played sardines? You go and hide somewhere in the house. Then the other players have to go and find you. When one person finds you they have to join you in the hiding place. This means that you could end up with 12 people trying to hide under a bed or 10 people in a fridge. 6 people all trying to get into a microwave is no fun, I can tell you!

I once played this game with a group of friends on a weekend away. I was sent to go and hide and they were going to come and find me. I have to admit I was quite pleased with myself as I had thought I had found the best place in the whole of the building. I had squeezed into a small opening in the wooden floor; as the trap door was so tiny I thought that I should give them a chance and keep the door open. Twenty-five minutes later no one had found me and I was bored. I realised that they had sent me off to wind me up, but this was not my only problem – I couldn't get back up out of the trap door. It was too high up off the ground that I was standing on and I couldn't even reach the floorboards. I hadn't fully thought through my plan of hiding or how I was going to get out. The building had been an old barn that had been renovated, and I was in an old coal store. I shouted and shouted but no one came – the stone walls were too thick – and I was too stuck to move.

Eventually, after a good hour, a friend came to find me in the hole and let me out – not using the trap door which I had gone through but by using the coal shute door which was a good metre wide.

If we are trapped or left to sit in a corner, it is very difficult to do anything useful. Like me trapped in the hole, if the Holy Spirit is left to sit hidden away in a Christian's life, he is unable to do anything, unable to challenge us or even help and guide us. Every Christian has the Holy Spirit but not every Christian allows him to move freely around their living room. In the Bible we are told to be filled with the Spirit so that we can become more like the One who created us.

What stops us from receiving the Holy Spirit?

God is an amazing God who always wants to help us and give us what we need. God is desperate to share his Spirit with us but sometimes we put things in his way to stop us being filled. For example:

1. We don't believe that we are worth such a cool gift.
2. We are scared that it may harm us.
3. Because we can't see it, we believe that it can't exist.
4. It's hard to hand over control of our life when we spend most of our time trying to gain control of it from teachers and family members.

God loves giving us gifts, and all his gifts are good. It's not about being worthy because none of us is worthy of anything God gives us. God promises to give his Spirit to anyone who asks.

'So I say to you: Ask and it will be given to you; seek and you will find; knock and the door will be opened to you. For everyone who asks receives; he who seeks finds; and to him who knocks, the door will be opened.' (Luke 11:9-13)

But this does not stop us being scared of what God's Spirit can do for us. Will it be all it's cracked up to be? Will it be as good as the Bible makes out?

Brum brum

Driving a car is one of the most exciting things I have ever learnt to do. I loved learning how to move from gear to gear, how to turn on the screen-washer and then how to turn it off again, and how to drive around a roundabout. In fact, I loved it so much I passed my test first time, even though I had a driving instructor I couldn't understand; when he said, 'Turn right', I thought he said, 'Get things right', so

I panicked and drove on to the motorway. Bad move as I had never been on a motorway before.

I love driving so much that you probably wouldn't believe that three months before I learnt to drive I almost decided not to bother. I had wanted to drive for so long that when the time had almost come, I started questioning what I needed to drive for. I was panicking that it was going to be too hard to learn. What if I couldn't do it? What if I couldn't remember what to do with all the bits? I know now that driving is dead easy: there is a wheel you turn and a start and stop pedal. There was no need to worry, but from the other side it looked like a mountain to climb and I couldn't imagine doing it.

Our fears sometimes stop us doing things that we might enjoy. Sometimes fear is good. Being scared of jumping off a cliff is a good fear because it would probably hurt a lot or we would die. But fear can be something that holds us back from things that will help us in life.

Placing the Holy Spirit in the centre of our lives should not be something that scares us; God is not going to let us down. God loves us and only wants the best. If we ask God to move into the centre of our living room of life, then that is what he will do. As he does this, he will bring with him all the wonderful gifts that the Spirit brings.

Going deeper

1. How do you feel about the Holy Spirit? Is it something there but distant, or something that is working within your life?

2. If you feel that you don't have the Holy Spirit, then why not write a list of things that are stopping you from getting to know him better? You could chat over with an older Christian the issues that you have.

3. How important do you think it is to see the Holy Spirit work before you buy into it?

4. Every Christian has the Holy Spirit but not all take full advantage. How could you help a Christian you know to use the Spirit to its full advantage?

5. Read 1 Corinthians 12:8-11. Do you have any of these gifts? Why not ask God to give you one of the gifts? Which would be the gift you would like the most?

6. Read though some of these verses about the Holy Spirit: Ephesians 1:17; Ezekiel 1:24; Luke 1:35; 1 John 5:6; Nehemiah 9:20; Isaiah 11:2. What are the different names for the Spirit, and what are the different things he does? What do you think is his main job?

QUESTION 9
Do I need a club card to become a Christian?

Becoming a Christian is easy once you have made the decision to do it. It took me 15 years to make the decision for myself but only moments to become a part of the family. I spent so long questioning, wanting to know what everyone else had and complaining, that I waited far too long. I decided to take the plunge and jump in the pool. Once I did everything changed.

Mr and Mrs Perfect

Too often you come across someone who thinks that they can't be a Christian because their life is too much of a mess at the moment. God loves messy people; you don't need to become perfect. You don't give yourself a wash before getting into the shower – what's the point?

I find people with cleaners funny. Even though the cleaner comes on Wednesdays, they always run around the house trying to tidy and pick up rubbish the night before. They clean the kitchen, hoover the rooms, empty the bins, wash the pots, put away all the clean washing, clean the windows and even the bath, but what's the point?

It's like going to the hairdresser. How often do you wash and style your hair before going to have it washed and cut? It's comical: you can watch young men, mums and grannies arriving for their routine haircut with perfectly styled hair – it's it quite obvious they've spent ages blow-drying it that morning.

People pay someone to wash their hair and it's already done. It's the same with God. We don't need to be sorted before we meet with him; we need to be real. If we keep putting off meeting with him because our lives are a mess, we will never get there. The truth is we are a mess and we will remain a mess until we let him sort us out.

Saying hello

The starting place for becoming a Christian is saying hello to our Maker. We sometimes think that becoming a Christian is hard, like filling in a form to become a member of the video shop where you need seven proofs of ID and four passport photos. The start is saying hi, telling God you're there and you're interested. You don't need to do it with religious language or in a religious-looking building; try saying hi the same way you would talk to a friend. What you say doesn't need to be well thought out but it does need to be well meant. God knows you, so be straight with him; try saying it as it is and as real as you can make it. You could try saying something like:

God, I'm interested in who you are and want to get to know you better. I know my life has been run by me making my own choices, but now could you help me live it in a way that makes me more like you. I thank you for your Son and for everything he has done for me. Please help me get to know you more each day.

Pass Go and collect £200

It's really as simple as that. Becoming a Christian isn't like joining any club where you are promised a £15 gift voucher or a toaster within a week if you fill in all the paperwork. Don't expect to get a club card and a constitution to sign; it doesn't really work like that. Becoming a Christian means that you have the knowledge of the great things to come in heaven (which may involve the £15 gift voucher and the toaster), but God is here with you now on this planet, helping and supporting you through the little as well as the big things in life.

Following Jesus is a fresh start, a new beginning. Think of it like an old leaf that is falling apart because it is so dry. Jesus didn't die to help us turn over a new leaf and start a new life with the same old dried-out lives, with hurt and pain still involved. Jesus died to give a whole new life –a whole new leaf, a new leaf that is no longer caught up with the pain and hurt that we once had.

People often think that Christianity is about keeping some old rules and going through religious rituals. Nothing could be further from the truth. Jesus said he had come so that we could have 'life to the full' – a life characterised not by religion but by freedom and security, purpose and power.

Freedom – from fear, guilt and the things we put in place to block our relationship with God.

Security – knowing that God loves us for who we are.

Purpose – because God has a plan for our lives and is determined to see it through.

Power – miraculous, supernatural, life-changing power as God becomes real in our lives.

So what now?

1. Take one day at a time. Becoming a Christian doesn't mean that you'll know all the answers straightaway; if you do, then God really has given you a miracle. You will make mistakes and wonder why you just can't seem to get it right. If you feel that you're losing a battle, then stop, take a deep breath and start again. God would rather see you try and fail than never try at all.

2. Try reading your Bible a little every day. Take it easy. If you started running a 10,000-metre race by running as fast as you could, by the time you got to the 300-metre marker you would be half-dead. In a long race you start by running at a slower pace,

and then, as you get closer to the end, you speed it up until you're running as fast as you can. Why kill yourself reading the Bible within the first few weeks? Start by reading a little each day and up the pace as time goes by. It's the same with prayer. Start slowly; pray for little things. Don't start out by jumping in and praying for world issues for hours on end. Build it up slowly; you will develop a stronger prayer life that way.

3. Let God tell you what you need to change, what things you will need to stop doing and what to start. All Christians are hoping to become more like God, and the only way this is going to happen is if we listen to what God sees is wrong with us.

4. If you don't know any already, get to know some Christians your own age. Maybe join a youth group or visit a church with young people in it. It is so easy when we first become Christians to slip back into our old lifestyle, but if we have Christians around us it's much easier to see where we are going wrong. All Christians need support. I have this great idea for a PPCP (Portable Pump-up Christian Pal). Whenever we are struggling all we'd have to do is pump up our PPCP and lean on them. I think it would sell millions, all those Christians finding support in a pump-up friend. The great thing is, we already have this device in the Christians around us: young Christian friends support each other in the same way the PPCP does, holding each other firm when times are tough.